Extreme Readers®

CONFIDENT
3
READER

Incredible Edibles

School Specialty
Publishing
Columbus, Ohio

By Teresa Domnauer

School Specialty.
Y Publishing

Copyright © 2007 School Specialty Publishing, a member
of the School Specialty Family.

Printed in the United States of America. All rights reserved. Except as permitted
under the United States Copyright Act, no part of this publication may be
reproduced or distributed in any form or by any means, or stored in a database or
retrieval system, without prior written permission from the publisher, unless
otherwise indicated.

Library of Congress Cataloging-in-Publication Data is on file with the publisher.

Send all inquiries to:
School Specialty Publishing
8720 Orion Place
Columbus, OH 43240-2111

ISBN 0-7696-4339-6

2 3 4 5 6 7 8 9 10 PHX 10 09 08

People eat different kinds of foods.
In some countries,
people enjoy eating snails.
In other places, seaweed soup makes
a delicious breakfast.
All around the world, there are
weird and wonderful things to eat!

Snails

In France, snails are a special
thing to eat.
A dish made with snails is
called *escargot* (ess-car-GO).
To make escargot, the snails are
taken out of their shells.
Then, they are cooked
with butter and other ingredients.

Weird Facts

- In France, people eat thousands of tons of snails each year.
- Snails were among the first animals that people ate.

Caviar

Caviar is a food made from fish eggs.
The eggs come from fish called *sturgeon*.
Caviar is never cooked.
It is usually served on small pieces of
toast or with tiny pancakes called *blini*.
Fine caviar is very expensive.

Weird Facts

- Some of the world's best caviar comes from Russia and Iran.
- Caviar should not be served with a metal spoon. It changes the taste. Special spoons of bone or tortoise shell are used to serve caviar.

Sushi

Sushi is a kind of food
that comes from Japan.
It is usually made of rice wrapped
in seaweed.
Some sushi has raw fish in it.
Salmon and tuna are two kinds of fish
used in sushi.
Sushi is served with soy sauce
and a spicy green topping called
wasabi (WA-sah-bee).

Weird Facts

- Some chefs study for many years
  to become master sushi chefs.

- The word *sushi* does not mean "raw fish."
  It describes the sticky rice used in sushi
  that has been cooked in vinegar.

Oysters

Oysters are a kind of shellfish.
Often, they are eaten raw.
Raw oysters are served in their shells
on ice.
Most people eat them with lemon
and a spicy sauce.
Oysters are wet and slippery.
They slide right down the throat!

Weird Facts

- Pearls are found inside some special oysters called *pearl oysters.*
- Many of the world's oyster farms are in the United States, South Korea, Japan, and France. People raise and sell oysters there.

Squid

A squid is a sea creature.
It is in the same animal family
as the octopus.
People all around the world eat squid.
Sometimes, squid is fried.
Other times, squid is cooked in
tomato sauce.
Squid is very chewy to eat.

Weird Facts

- Octopus is even chewier to eat than squid.
  It needs to cook for a long time to make it
  less chewy.

- A squid's arms and tentacles can be
  eaten, too!

13

Alligator

If you go to Louisiana in the southern United States, you can order alligator for lunch.
You can also buy alligator meat in the grocery store.
People use alligator in a kind of cooking called *Cajun*.
This type of cooking is very spicy.
People eat grilled alligator, fried alligator, and alligator stew!

Weird Facts

- Alligator does not taste fishy. It has a taste all its own. Some people say it tastes a little like chicken.

- Crocodile meat is also eaten in countries, such as Singapore, India, and Australia.

15

Insects

It may seem strange to eat insects.
But people have eaten insects
for thousands of years.
In Singapore or Thailand,
people eat ants.
In parts of Africa and South America,
people eat caterpillars.

Weird Facts

- Most insects are good for you. They are very high in protein and low in fat.

- In Mexico, over 300 different kinds of insects are used as food.

Tripe

Tripe is food made from the lining
of a cow's stomach.
Many people think it is delicious.
People use tripe to make soups
and stews.
It is eaten in many places in Europe.
Tripe can be found in most grocery
stores in the United States, too.

Weird Facts

- Tripe is an ingredient in some kinds
  of hot dogs.
- Tripe can be found in a Mexican soup
  called *menudo.*

Ostrich Eggs

The ostrich is the largest
bird in the world.
Its eggs are the largest in the world, too.
An ostrich egg is about the size
of a football.
One ostrich egg can make
scrambled eggs for ten people!

Weird Facts

- It takes 20 chicken eggs to make the same amount of food that one ostrich egg makes.

- Ostrich eggs have such tough shells that people use hammers to crack them open!

Fungi

Fungi are kinds of plants
that do not need sunshine to grow.
Mushrooms are a kind of fungus
that people eat.
People eat mushrooms all around
the world.
They put mushrooms in salad,
on pizza, in soups, and much more.

Weird Facts

- Many wild mushrooms are not safe to eat. Only experts should pick them for eating.
- Truffles are another kind of fungus that people eat. They grow underground and must be sniffed out by dogs or pigs.

Flowers

Many people eat the seeds from flowers,
such as sunflower seeds.

But many people eat the flowers
themselves, too!

Flowers, such as marigolds, daisies,
and roses, can be eaten.

People put flowers in soups and salads.

People also use flowers to make tea.

Be careful, though, since not all flowers
are good or safe to eat.

Weird Facts

- Some flowers, such as violets, can be frosted with sugar and used to decorate cakes.

- People grow some vegetables, such as artichokes and broccoli, for their edible flowers.

25

Seaweed

Seaweed is a plant found in oceans all around the world.
It can be used as food in many ways.
Japanese sushi is wrapped in sheets of dried seaweed.
People in Hawaii and Asia eat seaweed often.
They put it in soups and salads.
They also serve it with vegetables.

Weird Facts

- Seaweed is full of healthy vitamins and minerals.
- Seaweed is also used to make goods, such as toothpaste, paint, and soap.

Durian Fruit

This large, spiny fruit is a durian (DUR-ee-en) fruit.
It grows on trees in Southeast Asia.
Many people think the durian fruit is delicious.
But it has an awful smell!
People are not allowed to bring durian fruit inside many hotels, taxis, and airplanes.
This is because it smells so bad.

Weird Facts

- It can take as long as 15 years for a durian tree to grow fruit.
- The durian is one of the largest fruits in the world. It can weigh over ten pounds—as much as a bowling ball!

Food and Family

Food keeps people healthy and strong.
For many families around the world,
mealtime is a special part of the day.
It is a time when family members
can talk and relax together.
Families eat many different kinds
of food.
What kinds of food do you eat?

Weird Facts

- In South Africa, families eat puthu. Puthu is a kind of porridge made from corn.

- In India, families eat dal, a sauce made from lentils.

EXTREME FACTS ABOUT
INCREDIBLE EDIBLES!

- There are over 100 kinds of snails that can be eaten.
- The best caviar in the world is called *beluga caviar*. A very small amount of this caviar costs over 200 dollars!
- Eel, crab, and squid are popular fillings for sushi.
- Oysters have many vitamins and minerals.
- A black liquid, called *ink*, comes from squid. Sometimes, it is used to color pasta or rice.
- The tail of the alligator holds the best meat to eat. Tail meat is white and tender.
- In the Asian country of Laos, giant tarantulas are eaten as snacks.
- Italians serve tripe with tomato sauce, basil, and Parmesan cheese.
- People eat the meat of ostriches, as well as their eggs.
- Some mushrooms are so poisonous that eating them can cause death.
- The heads of dandelions can be made into coffee or wine.
- There are 10,000 different kinds of seaweed.
- In Singapore, signs at train stations warn people not to bring durian fruits on trains.
- In Thailand, quail eggs and fresh fish are part of family dinners.